Sacred Stillness

First published in 2025 by
Red Stripe Press
Dublin, Ireland
www.redstripepress.com

Paperback ISBN: 978-1-78605-270-4
ePub ISBN: 978-1-78605-271-1
Audiobook ISBN: 978-1-78605-290-2

Set in Tisa Pro, Tisa Sans Pro

Cover design and typesetting by www.typesetting.ie

Printed and bound in the EU

Sacred Stillness

A Book of Meditations from the Sanctuary

Compiled by
Sr Stan and Síle Wall

RS
Red Stripe Press

Acknowledgements

Firstly, we sincerely thank all the Sanctuary facilitators who so kindly and thoughtfully contributed to this book. We would like to thank Michael Brennan and Eileen O'Brien for their hard work in editing and publishing the book, and Benil Shah, for complimenting the beautiful words with beautiful imagery. A special thank you also to Kathleen Curley-Clarke for typing and coordinating the project.

Contents

Foreword

Be Still. Breathe Deeply. Be Present to the moment as it is. Open to the transcendent ground of all being. Dwell in gratitude. Stretch the body. Then, arise to serve all in compassion.

These are the beginning practices that arise whenever a human being looks within and asks questions of meaning. They teach simple lessons, each profound in their own way. Practiced together and with regularity they transform the daily experience of our lives. All the great wisdom traditions of the world know this, and though they may differ in their teachings in many respects, they all begin their inner practice from here. This is a lesson we have learned over the last twenty-five years in the Sanctuary Centre. Founded by Sr Stan and Síle Wall in the Christian tradition, but with a vision of openness to the wisdom of all traditions, it has become a place of peace, dialogue, and welcome to all, centred on these simple practices of meditative, mindful, compassionate awareness. This book arises from that vision. In it you will find many doors into stillness drawn from many traditions and teachers connected to the Sanctuary. May you find one, or more, that lead you into that depth of stillness in which we touch the truth at the centre of our being, the peace that passes understanding, the beauty that breathes compassion into your heart, and through your heart into a world so in need of it.

Be still and you will know.

Brother Richard

Introduction

This book offers real, practical, profound and creative meditation practices through a variety of themes and poems. It is a tapestry woven from the unique contributions of the many people, coming from different faiths and wisdom traditions, who are part of the Sanctuary. Each meditation is like an open door, inviting the reader or the listener with insightful ways to connect, or reconnect, with an experience of stillness. In a world filled with constant noise and distractions, discovering stillness is a sacred experience.

Each person invited to contribute to this book responded positively and without hesitation. Each practice is intentionally crafted. Deep personal thought, reflection and inner wisdom can be sensed under the various themes. The essence of the Sanctuary is embodied throughout.

These meditations are for everyone – from the beginner to the long-time practitioner – for all seekers and searchers. It can be used in a multitude of ways, from the ancient wisdom meditation traditions of focusing on the breath, through to reading, listening, journaling or reflecting.

Our hope is that these meditations and poems will evoke a stirring of your heart, bringing you into a closer relationship with yourself, the world you are part of and your God, offering you a pathway into stillness where you will find sanctuary.

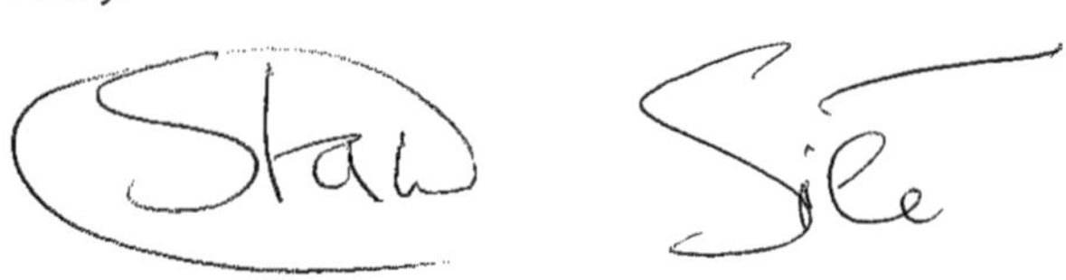

Ways to Practise

Time and Place

To introduce, cultivate and deepen your meditation practice, you need to give time to it regularly. We suggest that you start by carving ten minutes out of each day. Morning is usually best, but you can choose the time of day that suits you. Over time, you may work up to twenty or thirty minutes. This may mean sacrificing something else, for example, some extra time asleep, or in conversation, listening to the radio or scrolling a screen.

You also need to find a quiet space in which to meditate. We believe this is essential for all of us because of the hectic pace of life and the noise that invades our lives today. It doesn't matter where the space is, as long as it is a quiet place for you.

Towards the end of your meditation time, we suggest that you spend a few moments reflecting on any thoughts, moods, feelings, sensations, realisations or curious points of interest that are stirred in your heart during meditation – just becoming aware of what is happening within you and around you.

Breathing

We suggest that you start each quiet time by allowing yourself to connect with your own breath. If you find it difficult to quieten down, to be truly present to each moment, we suggest you use your breath to slow your mind and move into your body. Concentrate on the breath: in and out, easy and regular. Breathe easily and regularly and attentively.

Focusing on your breath can help you move into that quiet space within you, where you will find moments of inner stillness. The following are some pointers:

- Notice how breath and body connect
- Allow this movement to be as it is
- The mind is always busy
- Call it back with the breath
- Breathe in for three, out for three
- Breathe in for four, breathe out for six
- Reflect

Reading

When you are at peace in your quiet space, we suggest that you choose one of the meditations – whichever one appeals to you at the time. Listen to or read some or all of the text, slowly. Even a few lines at a time, or one word – whatever you feel drawn to – can speak to you. It may help to repeat a few lines aloud to yourself, so you can hear the words, feel them as well as read them. Allow the words a place to rest within.

- Read a line, a verse, or focus on just one word
- Listen to what speaks to you
- Pause
- Reflect

Journaling

Keeping a journal of any kind can offer a creative way of moving into stillness. Writing or art making, just for yourself, can be used as a record to look back on, at the end of each day, week, month or year. Words or images that arise gently open the heart and help integrate your life experience into your practice.

- Write
- Use colour
- Make marks
- Look
- Reflect

A Doorway into Stillness

Dominic Cogan

Being busy commands respect in the contemporary world. But the natural world around us invites to be still. Stillness can become a doorway into the realm of the sacred.

Meditation

Being still is an achievement.
Cats, frogs, spiders and many other animals and insects
appear to do it effortlessly.
Trees and other plants
are particularly called to stillness, even when touched by a breeze.
Within every twenty-four-hour cycle we are all drawn into the stillness of sleep. The French seventeenth-century philosopher Blaise Pascal is reputed to have said that 'All of humanity's problems stem from our inability to sit quietly in a room.' This is something worth pondering.

Stillness, is a doorway into the sacred,
setting us apart from the busyness of the everyday.
With the body at rest and the feet in contact with the floor
we may close the eyes.
We are not trying to go to sleep.
We are allowing our attention to shift
from what we see outwardly with our eyes.
Now letting the inner eye of the heart
become alive
to what is going on inside of us.

Taking some time to tune into the body.
Noting any tiredness or excitement.
Sensing any tightness or discomfort.
Becoming aware of any traces of ease, of openness in the body.
Allowing the body to simply be as it is.
Similarly, taking note of the activity of the mind.
Allowing it to be just as it is,
adopting an attitude of quiet observance.
Let thoughts come and go.
Observe them arrive and depart.

Now, gently explore the inner weather patterns of the heart.
As best you can,
welcoming or at least allowing whatever is here to be:

boredom, joy, excitement, sadness, anxiety, anger,
contentment.
Just as the tree and the blade of grass
bend to the energy of the wind without resistance,
we just sit and let it all happen.
Quietly observing,
quietly opening the door,
allowing
the possibility of stillness to emerge within.
Letting things be just as they are.
Responding to the deep inner calling, to just be.
This is not the stillness of immobility.
This is the sacred stillness that replenishes the heart.
As the heart quietens,
it has the capacity to unfold.

As this meditation comes to its close,
opening to the sacred stillness all around you
and within.

Stillpoint

Contemplation happens when,
seduced by longing,
we let go our grasp
of our well-constructed
temples of defence and security
abandoning ourselves –
all naked and unknowing –
to the pursuit
of the hunger in our guts.
Ah, then,
when all our bright masks
are left aside
we fall into
ourselves,
perhaps to meet there,
all cradled by emptiness –

the Stillpoint
rooting us in divinity
and washing us over in deep, deep peace.

Edwina Gateley

(from Edwina Gateley and Jane Hammond-Clarke (2000), *Whispers: Conversations with Edwina Gateley*, Trabuco Canyon, CA: Source Books)

A Soft Landing

Orla Burchael

This meditation is based on the work of Bonnie Badenoch, Nurturing the Heart with the Brain in Mind, *and on Taoist meditation practices. The weaving together of ancient wisdom traditions with findings of modern neuroscience is rich and I find this to be a really deep practice.*

The practice focuses on embodiment and the expansion of compassionate non-judgemental awareness. This is the grounds for safety as we relate to ourselves, others and the wider world. The practice can be used as a soft landing or mindful check in at the beginning or end of the day, or indeed at transitions throughout the day.

Meditation

Finding a comfortable position with feet touching the ground.
Gently closing your eyes or lowering your gaze so your eyelids are resting.

Opening to the possibility of settling, arriving in this moment.
Bringing your attention to this breathing body.
Doing a gentle scan from your head down to the feet.
Particularly paying attention to the soles of the feet that always have a special connection with the Earth, which offers great stability.
Just as the trees, flowers and shrubs have roots, you too can have roots that go down into the Earth.
Just imagining roots emerging from the soles of your feet, deepening and spreading into the Earth.
Roots offer structure, stability, solidity – but also nourishment.
Allowing for the possibility of nourishment being absorbed through your roots from the Earth,
Nourishment, finding its way to wherever it is needed in the body.
Gently moving your awareness from the feet to your legs,
particularly to the quality of the muscles.
The muscles can tell us a lot about how we are.
So, deeply listening to your legs.
Do they feel strong, shaky or achy?
Is it possible to allow whatever you find, to be there,
bringing a compassionate and kind awareness?
Gently moving your awareness to the abdomen.
This is the belly mind or the belly brain.

On a physical level, this part of the body is involved in the wonderful process of nourishment, digestion and assimilation of food.
But, on many other levels it is involved in the processing of experiences, relationships and all that is happening in this moment.
The belly mind is the guardian of our safety.
If we listen to it, it will always tell us how we are,
particularly our level of safety in this moment.
Gently listening for what is here through the language of sensation,
allowing whatever you find.
Honouring the wisdom of the belly mind, the guardian of our safety.
Now, bringing your awareness to the heart area.
This is the heart mind or the heart brain.
On a physical level, it is an amazing organ that pumps oxygenated blood to every single cell and organ.
On other levels the heart is the great connecter.
Take a few moments to listen to the heart.
Sometimes the heart is very open to connection
but at other times, in its wisdom, it is in a more tender and protective mode.
Now, gently moving our awareness to the neck and the shoulders.
Listening to the muscles of the neck and shoulders, which are always communicating.

Also listening to the muscles of the jaw.
Listening as if to a dear friend.
Moving up now to muscles beside the eyes, which tighten when we are stressed and soften when we are safe and belong.
Listening with a compassionate and non-judgemental awareness.
Now moving to the wonderful skull brain.
Bringing a hand to the forehead, the thinking brain.
The other hand to the instinctual brain at the base of the skull.
Offering some attention to this wondrous part of us.
Perhaps the head is heavy with thoughts.
Offering some reassurance.
And finally becoming aware of the expansiveness above,
the heavens, planetary bodies and spiritual energies.
Human beings and all living things exist between Heaven and Earth for our whole lives and are nurtured by both.

'I park, pause, take heed.
Breathe. Just breathe and sit ...'

Seamus Heaney, from 'The Blackbird of Glanmore'

Acceptance

Richard Bohan Martin

Acceptance isn't about agreeing with everything that happens. It's about no longer adding suffering to suffering – about meeting life with an open heart, even when it's hard. If judgement arises, meet it with tenderness. If fear appears, let it be there without following it. You are not your thoughts. You are the awareness that holds them.

Meditation

Begin by settling in, just as you are.
There's nowhere else to be, nothing else to do.
Let the weight of striving soften, even for just these few
moments.
Now, bring to mind a simple phrase,
like a quiet offering to yourself:
May I meet this moment with acceptance.
No need to force it.
No need to believe it fully.

Just let the words be an invitation,
a reminder that you are worthy of your own kindness,
exactly as you are.
Perhaps you notice resistance,
a tightness, a thought that says, 'I shouldn't feel this way'?
That's okay.
Instead of turning away,
see if you can offer that resistance a bit of space.
Like holding a child's hand, gently, without pulling or pushing.
You might whisper
It's alright.
This, too, belongs.
Meeting this moment with acceptance.

Now, picture someone who may be struggling.
Offer them the same wish: *May you meet this moment with acceptance.*
Feel how the heart naturally softens when you wish others well.
We all struggle.
We all long to be at peace.
Rest in this knowing.
Acceptance is a practice, not a finish line.
It's alright.
This, too, belongs.
Meeting this moment with acceptance.

Courageous Rest

Some of us
need to discover
that we will not begin
to live
more fully
until we have the
courage to do and see
and taste and experience
much less than usual ...
There are times
when in order to keep
ourselves in existence at
all we simply have to sit
back for a while and
do nothing. And for a person
who has let themself be

drawn completely out of
themselves by their activity,
nothing is more difficult
than to sit still and rest,
doing nothing at all.
The very act of resting is
the hardest and most
courageous act a person can
perform.

Thomas Merton

Arriving into Stillness

John Doherty

This practice is based on the idea of holding a container of loving kindness and awareness for ourselves and our story. The more we hold this space the more we experience being held by the wider spiritual container around and within us.

Meditation

Find a comfortable posture that feels stable and at ease.

Arriving in Stillness

Take a deep breath in ... and gently exhale.
Allow yourself to settle into this moment, into your body, into your breath.
Bring to mind the image of a container – your own inner space of awareness. This container holds all of you, just as you are.
It is a space of calm, of presence, of acceptance.

Inviting Inner Stillness

As you breathe, invite your inner winds to settle, your inner storms to quiet.
There is nothing to force, nothing to fix – just the simple act of allowing.
Stillness is not something we create; it is something we uncover.
Your role is not to make it happen,
but simply to hold this container of awareness with loving kindness.
Breathe deeply into your body.
Let the breath bring you home to the present moment.
With each inhale, feel yourself arriving more fully here.
With each exhale, let go of any tension, any resistance.

Observing with Kindness

The mind always seeks a task, so give it a gentle one: simply observe.
Notice the sensations in your body.
Are there any areas of tension – your jaw, your shoulders, your neck?
If so, allow them to soften.
Give yourself permission to rest in awareness.
This is a practice of being.
Nothing to do, nothing to achieve.
Just being here, with yourself, in kindness and presence.

Opening to the Greater Field

As you rest in awareness, begin to open to something larger – the vast field of spiritual presence that surrounds and holds you.
There is no separation between you and this field.
The container of your awareness and the spaciousness of existence are one.
Breathe into this unity.
Let yourself surrender, not as a giving up, but as an opening – a merging into the greater awareness that is always here.

Returning with Presence

As you move toward closing this practice
let yourself rest in this space.
Allow whatever arises to be held in the container of your awareness.
And now, taking a deep breath in ...
Gently begin to reconnect to the room you are in.
Stretch if you'd like; move your body in a way that feels natural.
When you are ready, return, bringing this awareness with you.

'I know of no other single thing so conducive to misery as an uncultivated and untrained mind.
I know of no other single thing so conducive to happiness as a cultivated and well-trained mind.'

The Buddha

Attention

Mairead O'Keefe

Meditation

Bringing attention to the shape of your resting body.
Feeling the edges and curves of the body.
Perhaps you can notice the contact of your hands with each other,
or with your body?
Maybe the contact of the air against your skin?

Directing your attention more inwards now, with curiosity,
noticing sensations in the body.
Perhaps tingling, throbbing, pulsing, numbness, itchiness, aches or other sensations?
Are there parts of the body that feel tight, tense, light or spacious?
Bringing awareness to these sensations,
maybe they get stronger or weaker, or fade away?

Just paying attention.
Noticing, too, when the mind begins to wander into thinking.
This is normal.
It's difficult for our attention to stay focused on one thing,
for any length of time.
If you are noticing this happening,
bring a gentle, kindly, friendly attention
to your present moment experience.

I now invite you to shift your attention from sensations to sounds,
becoming aware of the soundscape.
Not thinking about the sounds or trying to identify them,
just allowing them to arrive.
There may be sounds from inside the body,
sounds from inside the room,
sounds from outside.
Becoming aware of
subtle sounds,
louder sounds,
occasional sounds,
continuous sounds.
Noticing gaps between sounds,
maybe noticing the sound of silence?
Bringing a gentle, kindly, friendly attention
to your present moment experience.

Coming towards the close of this practice,
becoming aware of your breathing.
Feeling the waves of breath throughout your body.
Paying attention, just being present.
Grateful for the beauty and detail of being mindfully present.
Grateful for the gift of attention.

Silence

I catch the pattern
Of your silence
Before you speak

I do not need
To hear a word.

In your silence
Every tone I seek
Is heard.

Langston Hughes

Beauty Through the Senses

Aurora Procopio

To me, beauty is the manifestation of the Divine presence on Earth. Beauty isn't just an external quality but something we perceive with all our senses and carry within ourselves. Beauty is in the way we experience life, in the harmony of nature, in art, in kindness and in moments of stillness.

Meditation

I invite you to find a quiet place in nature,
a place where nobody can disturb you for the next short while.
This place can be a forest, your local park or community garden,
your backyard garden or just looking at the space outside your window.
Once you are there,
I invite you to find a posture that allows you to feel alert, engaged and awake.

Maybe you are experiencing a sense of the energy around,
knowing that the sky is above and the Earth beneath.
Slowly, turn your attention to the breath,
taking a few breaths in through the nose and out through the mouth,
allowing Mother Earth to receive your breath as you breathe out.
I invite you to turn your attention to the sense of touch.
Notice the way the air touches you.
Notice the temperature, perhaps the warmth of sunlight or a gentle breeze on your face.
Now, move your attention to the sense of smell.
As you breathe through the nose, notice what kind of scents this place is offering.
See if you can pick up any subtle scents around,
perhaps the freshly cut grass or the wild flowers.
Become aware of sound.
Notice any nearby sounds, distant sounds, and any sounds in between.
What do you hear?
Perhaps the birds chatting, the rustling of leaves or the wind whispering.
Gently begin to notice the space around you,
noticing the colours, shapes and patterns.
What do you see?
Perhaps the vast sky, the sunset, the trees,
maybe birds flying or a butterfly.

Taking in all or some of your sense experiences,
I invite you now to take a moment just to appreciate the sacred and ever-present beauty that is offered every day, in any given and precious moment of life.

'People say that what we're all seeking is a meaning for life. I don't think that's what we're really seeking. I think that what we're seeking is an experience of being alive, so that our life experiences on the purely physical plane will have resonances with our own innermost being and reality so that we actually feel the rapture of being alive.'

Joseph Campbell

Beauty Within

Aurora Procopio

Beauty exists in every moment of our lives; we just need to be still enough to notice it. It is reflected in our resilience, compassion and kindness. Beauty lives in our stories, in our courage, in the strength we show during difficult times and in the warmth of our smile.

Meditation

I invite you to find a quiet place where you can be quiet and still for the next while.
Choose a posture that feels relaxed and open.
Allow any tense areas of the body to soften.
Place your attention on the breath,
connecting with its flow and rhythm.

As you breathe, take a moment to recall a time when you learned something for the first time.

Maybe it was as a child, when you learned to ride a bike,
feeling a bit fearful or excited,
or perhaps it was the first time you swam.
As you recall this time, simply notice what arises for you as
you experience this memory:
emotions, sensations or thoughts.
As you continue to be here, quiet and still,
I invite you to bring to mind a time when you were kind to
somebody.
This can be a small act of kindness,
perhaps you offered to pick up some groceries for your
neighbour
or walked your friend's dog.
As you spend some time with this memory,
notice what kind of emotions, sensations and thoughts are
present.

Dropping these memories now, come back to the flow and
rhythm of the breath.
Connect to the beauty of you as a person, in this moment.
Connect to the essence of your being,
noticing the unique qualities that make you who you are,
the different expressions of your mind and heart,
your individuality,
the ways you express love, warmth and compassion.
Recognise that beauty is not something to chase,

beauty is always here and lives in every moment of our
breathing.
Beauty is within.
Beauty is reflected as our personal story
reminding us of who we are and the life we carry within.

Be Still Now

I walked along the western shore
One bright November day
I watched the heron watching me
And thought I heard him say

Just be still now
Wait a while
And let life come to you
Just be still now
All your dreams
Are on the breezes passing through

I walked along the city streets
And wished that I could fly
I saw the heron by my feet
And thought I heard him say

Just be still now
Wait a while
And let love come to you
Just be still now
All your dreams
Are on the breezes passing through

Just be still now
Just be still

Luka Bloom

Begin Again

Mary Jennings

We can begin again at any time in our meditation practice. That simple lesson also applies to life: we can begin again, letting go of the past, letting go of the future, letting go of the wandering mind – living now.

Meditation

Begin by settling into where you are right now,
checking that your spine is upright, without tension.
Become aware of your feet.
Become aware of your breath.
The in breath and the out breath, in breath and out breath.
You might notice any sounds within the space and then
sounds further away, letting them come to you, not
straining in any way.
Notice where your hands are and what they are touching –
the texture and feel of touch.
Be aware of the whole body, just here, gently breathing,

allowing sounds to be just here.
There is nothing to do right now, but be in this body,
this body gently breathing.
You might notice the wandering mind.
Observe thoughts appearing and disappearing,
coming and going, like clouds in the sky.
Be aware if you are getting caught up in any particular thought,
about the past, or the future.
When you become aware that you are getting snagged on any particular thought or memory,
come back to the breath
to begin again,
to be fully aware in this moment.
The in breath, followed by the out breath, and the slight pause in between.
That is all there is to do right now.
Be aware and alive in this moment, the body here, gently breathing.
No matter how many times your mind wanders, simply begin again.
The past is past. The future is not yet here.
There is only this moment.
Having the breath and the body as an anchor
to be in this only moment, this present moment.
Mindfulness is knowing where you are at any one moment.
If the mind has wandered away, begin again.

Begin again with a sense of kindness towards yourself.
No reproach, no harsh judgement.
Simply returning to the present moment.
Simply being mindful.

To begin again is a practice that can be cultivated,
become part of mindfulness practice,
become part of life.
To begin again is a gift we can give to ourselves,
right now in this moment and in any moment.
Begin.

Being with Pain

Tony Bates

Emotional pain is a messenger from a part of us that has no other way to communicate. Meditation is one way that can help us tune in, listen, hear, be with and open to pain, rather than pushing it away.

Meditation

Take time to breathe and steady yourself.
Allow your breath to earth you back into this moment.

Notice the weather around you,
the sky, the temperature, the colours, the people.
Allow what is present to be just as it is.

Close your eyes.
If it feels right, notice your inner emotional weather.
Be very gentle with yourself.
You don't need to 'take on' all your pain in one sitting.

Take time to breathe and steady yourself.
Allow your breath to earth you back into this moment.

Open your heart, in silence, to any pain within.
Welcome it as a part of yourself.
Your pain is seeking the tenderness of your attention.
Take a moment to acknowledge its presence.
Strong emotions need time to run their course before they settle.
Notice any change when you stop fighting with your pain.
Something shifts when we accept whatever is happening inside us
without judging it or rushing to 'fix' it.
Hold your pain in compassionate awareness
and notice a softening within.

Take time to breathe and steady yourself.
Allow your breath to earth you back into this moment.

If it feels right, open more deeply to your pain,
Notice where in your body you feel discomfort.
Breathe into that place and soften any tension around your pain.
With each in breath, welcome whatever arises.
With each out breath, release tension.
Give your emotions room to breathe.
Be gentle with yourself.

Maybe notice a softening within,
a shift that whispers of understanding and compassion.
When we hold pain in compassionate awareness
pain unfolds in a different way.

Take time to breathe and steady yourself.
Allow your breath to earth you back into this moment.

Just as you can move towards your pain,
it's equally important to allow yourself
to move back from your distress.
Without denying there is something in you
that wants to heal.

Take time to breathe and steady yourself.
Allow your breath to earth you back into this moment.

... back to your sitting in this room.
Slowly, in your own time, open your eyes
and notice where you are.

'In meditation, we take steps to achieve stillness. We quieten our bodies and our emotions, then, gradually allow the mind to become single-pointed. Stillness within one individual can affect society beyond measure.'

Father Bede Griffiths

Breathing with the Earth

Jean Barrett

As we turn toward our breath, we turn toward life itself. Each inhale, each exhale – an unbroken rhythm, carrying us through this existence. Breath is life and, in each moment, we have the opportunity to stop, to appreciate, to be fully present with the miracle of being alive.

Meditation

Pausing, bringing awareness to the breath.
Feeling it move through the body, sensing its presence.
Noticing how it feels,
the cool inhale, the warm exhale – the steady rise and fall,
a rhythm that has carried us since the moment we arrived in
this world.
When we connect with our breath, we connect with all of life.
Breath is not separate from the world around us,
it is woven into the very fabric of existence.
Breathing in, we take in what the trees offer us.

Breathing out we return our breath to them.
A sacred exchange.
A reminder that we are part of something vast,
held within the great pulse of life itself.
Nature breathes with us,
deepening our appreciation of life's unfolding.
Each season, each moment,
an invitation to pause, to open our senses fully.
Seeing the vibrant greens of spring.
Feeling the warmth of summer.
Touching the golden glow of autumn leaves.
Inhaling the crisp air of winter.
The breath of the world is all around us,
always moving, always present.
With each breath,
we honour the life within and around us.
Grounded in presence,
we embrace the beauty of this moment,
open,
connected,
at peace.

Chakras

Nikki Solyom

Meditation

Chakras are energy centres in the body identified by the Vedic practitioners throughout deep meditation practices. These centres align, unlock and release our power from within for balance in life.

Find a comfortable position and close your eyes. Take a deep breath in, letting the air fill your lungs, and exhale slowly, releasing any tension. Do this a few times, grounding yourself in the present moment.

Root Chakra (The Roots of the Tree)

Imagine yourself as a strong oak tree, with roots growing deep into the Earth. Visualise a red light at the base of your spine, like the sturdy roots that anchor you, providing stability and safety.

Affirmation:

I am grounded. I am safe. I am supported by the Earth.

Sacral Chakra (The Trunk of the Tree)

Shift your focus to your lower abdomen, the trunk of the tree. See a vibrant orange light here, like the trunk that supports your growth. Feel the creative energy flowing freely through you, nourishing your being.

Affirmation:

I embrace my creativity. I am open to joy and vitality.

Solar Plexus Chakra (The Strong Core of the Tree)

Visualise a bright yellow light in your solar plexus, the heart of your tree's strength. Feel your confidence growing like the tree's sturdy core, empowering you to stand tall.

Affirmation:

I am confident. I trust my inner strength.

Heart Chakra (The Heart of the Tree)

Bring your awareness to the centre of your chest, the tree's heart. Visualise a green light glowing, like the leaves of the oak tree, filled with love, compassion, and healing.

Affirmation:

I am love. My heart is open, nurturing all.

Throat Chakra (The Branches of the Tree)

Focus on your throat, the branches of your tree. See a calming blue light here, like branches reaching outward, expressing your truth with clarity and strength.

Affirmation:

> *I speak my truth. My voice is clear and strong.*

Third Eye Chakra (The Tree's Inner Wisdom)

Visualise an indigo light between your eyebrows, like the wisdom that flows through the tree's inner rings. Trust your intuition, as the tree trusts the flow of nature.

Affirmation:

> *I trust my intuition. I am guided by wisdom.*

Crown Chakra (The Top of the Tree)

Finally, visualise a violet or white light at the top of your head, the tree's crown reaching into the sky. Feel your connection to the heavens, to universal energy and Divine wisdom.

Affirmation:

> *I am one with the sky. I am connected to Divine wisdom.*

See all seven lights shining brightly. You are like an oak tree fully rooted in the Earth and reaching toward the sky. Feel the energy flowing freely and harmoniously through you, strong and balanced.

Affirmation to close:

I am grounded. I am strong. I am connected to the Earth and the sky.

Now Is the Time

Now is the time to know
That all that you do is sacred.

...

Now is the time for the world to know
That every thought and action is sacred.

This is the time
For you to deeply compute the impossibility
That there is anything
But Grace.

Now is the season to know
That everything you do
Is sacred.

Hafiz

(Edited from 'Now Is The Time', in Ladinsky, D. (1999) *The Gift: Poems Inspired by Hafiz, the Great Sufi Master*, London: Penguin.)

Cultivating Gratitude

Ailish Jameson

Core to my life is being able to reflect each morning and each evening on the positives in each day. Some days this can be more difficult than others due to the nature of our lives. But each morning when I wake up, I say 'thank you' for the fact that I am alive, am breathing, have a cosy bed and am safe. This is something that I started many years ago and it is now ingrained in my life. Every night before I go to sleep, I reflect on the day in totality and again give thanks, even in the most challenging of days, for my physical health, my breath and the people in my life. Starting and ending each day on a positive note has been transformative.

Meditation

Allowing yourself time to tune into the breath within your
body,
the rise and fall of the chest area, the ribcage, the shoulders,
and the air going in through the nose and out through the
mouth.

The breath is something we often take for granted,
yet, we are reliant on it.
Experiencing the breath moving in and out of the body.
Taking a moment to be thankful for the breath.
Bringing a sense of gratitude for this breath,
and the next breath,
and the next breath.
Noticing with each inhalation and exhalation,
how this movement is without effort.
Bringing gratitude to each rise and fall of the body as you breathe.
Focusing on gratitude.
Developing a 'gratitude attitude'.
Becoming aware of all that is good in this moment,
no matter how small.
Appreciating the value of everyday experiences.
At any point, if you find it difficult to focus
or notice the mind wandering off, which it often does,
gently bring the attention back to the breath.

Coming towards the end of this short practice,
take some time allowing a sense of a 'gratitude attitude' to be the primary focus.
Asking yourself the following questions:
What was one positive thing about my day today?
It can be the smallest of things, for example, your car started this morning,

you enjoyed a coffee with a valued friend,
you noticed the sunrise or the sunset.
What is key here is that it does not have to be anything grandiose or big; it starts with the simplest thing.
What was that experience like?
Perhaps at the time you may not have noticed it for its value
but looking back on it now,
what was so positive about it?
Why is that the experience that you are grateful for?

When we start to bring gratitude into our lives, we begin to recognise the positives and value in the moment rather than having to reflect on it afterwards.

'Silence is an ocean. Speech is a river. When the ocean is searching for you, don't walk into the river. Listen to the ocean.'

Rumi

Cultivating Inner Wisdom Through Holding Polarities

Anna Przybylo

Our body holds wisdom, which is our guide to cultivating presence, connection and authenticity. When we turn inwards to give attention to our inner experiences, we are invited to listen to the messages from within, honour them and learn from them. The more guided we are by our inner wisdom, the closer we feel to our true self.

This meditation is a pendulation practice rooted in somatic psychology where you are invited to hold the polarities within you. We all have experiences of both hurt and hope in our lives. We all have moments of contraction and expansion.

Meditation

As you settle into the practice,
take a moment to reflect upon a time of struggle,
experience of darkness, or pain.

This might be something from your past or from the present moment.

Then take a moment to recall a feeling of hope or connection.
This might be a time when you felt cared for,
were truly accepted for who you were.
It might be deep gratitude from within your heart.

Let one of your hands represent the pain or the struggle
and the other hand represent the hope.
Hold your hands in front of your chest as if they were holding both experiences.
Allow your attention to alternate like a pendulum between the two.
Your attention shifting between hurt and hope,
between contraction and expansion.

Now, slowly start exploring what it is like to bring your palms closer together. You might even bring them together.
Connect with the wisdom of your body, in this moment,
maybe asking yourself the question:
What is arising as I hold these polarities together?
Can they co-exist, without excluding each other?

Feel free to journal on your experience.

Distracted Parts and a Skilful Teacher

Barry Lee

A friend of mine works as a nature mentor for young people. He brings groups of children into the wilderness and teaches them how to track, forage for food, build shelters and make fire. These children are quite a diverse group, aged between 8 and 15. It's not easy! In most conventional classrooms, the teacher might say, 'Now children. We're learning maths. Everyone pay attention!' Control is imposed. Attention is demanded or coerced. I remember so many days in school, being that child who didn't want to pay attention ... who simply couldn't pay attention.

My friend is a different kind of teacher. When he is teaching young people how to build a fire, he just starts building a fire. That is the focus of his attention. He carefully clears the space, collects kindling and starts building the fire. Because he is fully present, at least one or two of the children are curious: 'What are you doing? Can I help?' Many others aren't interested yet. Some might be preoccupied with another game. Some might be too tired and might be resting. Some might have too much energy to sit still. My friend doesn't fight with them. He doesn't say, 'Everyone, get over here and pay attention!' He leaves them be. He lets them play or be distracted. He stays gathered and steady in himself and the small group continues working on the fire. More and more children are intrigued: 'What is going on over there?!' By the end, most of the group have settled and are happily learning about making a fire. I have seen this happen.

It's a lesson I try to bring into my own meditation practice.

Meditation

When I sit, very often there are parts of me that don't want to practise.
Just like the children in the forest,
there are parts that are distracted,
that are restless,
that are worried,
that are exhausted.
I think of my friend.
'I'm just going to sit here and breathe', I say.
'It's okay if you're too tired or distracted ... you don't have to pay attention', I say to my parts.
I feel my feet on the floor and my bum on the cushion.
I notice the subtly pleasant sensation of breathing in and breathing out.
That's all.
'If you would like to sit and breathe with me for a moment, you are welcome,' I say to my parts.

I'm not fighting with myself or scolding myself for not paying attention.
Maybe there is a feeling of relief,
a coming together, a sense of integration?
Usually by the end, all the parts are sitting together in practise.

'Silence is the language of God;
all else is poor translation.'

Rumi

Embodiment: Head and Face

Miriam Hurley

This meditation is a great way to relieve tension in the head and face. Mostly I don't realise when my brow is furrowed and my lips are pressed tightly together for no particular reason. This meditation can be done anytime, even in the middle of a conversation. It is an exercise that can be done sitting or standing.

Meditation

So, finding a comfortable but alert posture.
Having the feet flat on the floor with the back erect but not rigid.
Allowing for the natural curves of the spine
and directing your attention to the head and face.
Feeling how the neck lifts up out of the shoulders
with the head balancing on top of the neck,
effortless dignity.
Feeling into the head, the whole head.

Feeling from the inside out,
not visualising or thinking
really *feeling* the head and neck as best you can
on the surface and deeper.
Now, when you are ready bringing your awareness to the face,
the facial expression.
Focusing on the jaws and the mouth.
What sensations are here?
Tuning in to the lips.
Allowing them to be soft with the upper lip resting gently on the lower.
Directing your attention to the inside of the mouth,
the gums and teeth.
Focusing on the tongue,
allowing it to be relaxed the tip resting gently behind the upper incisors.
Becoming aware of the nose.
The tip of the nose and the nostrils,
the cheeks and the cheekbones.
Bringing the awareness to the ears and the ear canals.
Shifting the focus of your attention to the eyes,
the eye sockets, the eyeballs, the eye lids,
the eyebrows and the space between the eyebrows.
Tuning in to the temples and forehead.
What sensations are here, if any?
There could be tingling or itch,
a sense of ease or no sensations at all.

Focusing on the scalp,
the top of the head and the back of the head,
the skull beneath the skin and the brain inside the skull.
Broadening awareness
to include the space around the head and face,
and holding all this in a large, spacious awareness,
as best you can.
Now the invitation is to open the eyes,
if they've been closed,
broadening your awareness to include the space you are in right now.

Embodiment: Standing and Tilting

Miriam Hurley

The reason I like this meditation so much is that it is simple and accessible. I find it really effective in helping me to be in my body, giving my thinking mind a break. It is also very calming but also energising.

Meditation

Standing with the feet flat on the ground.
Having a sense of the legs rising up strongly to the pelvis.
As best you can, having the back erect but not rigid.
Gathering your awareness into a sense of the whole body
standing,
in an erect, relaxed posture.
A sense of being centred.

Now tuning in to the spine.
Feeling how it starts at the sacrum,
rises up out of the pelvis

to the shoulders and shoulder blades.
Allowing the shoulder joints to open and soften, as best you can.
Bringing your awareness to the neck,
the head balancing on top of the neck.

Becoming aware of the feet on the ground.
Really feeling the contact here,
the toes and the soles of the feet.
Then, with feet fully planted on the ground,
allowing the body to tilt slightly forward
so that most of the weight is in the balls of the feet.
Feeling how the muscles of the legs work to stop you from falling forward.
Maybe, feeling the kneecap and the muscles above the knee.
Directing your attention to the calves and the shins,
bringing your awareness to any and all sensations here.

When you are ready, moving back to centre.
Noticing any difference in sensations in the legs.
The mind will most likely move away from being with the body.
Whenever you notice this, just bringing you awareness back to the body.
A part of the body you have chosen as an anchor,
maybe the whole body.

Returning now to the contact of the feet with the ground.
Feeling how the ground supports you.
This time, allowing the body to lean slightly back
so the body weight is mostly in the heels,
with the feet again fully on the ground.
This time noticing
if different muscles are working to keep you upright.
Perhaps focusing on the muscles of the fronts of the thighs,
seeing what is to be noticed here.
What sensations are here?

Coming back to centre again
returning to an upright stance.
Having a sense of the whole body and the space around the body.

Wonder

Lord, purge our eyes to see
Within the seed a tree,
Within the glowing egg, a bird,
Within the shroud, a butterfly.
Till, taught by such we see,
Beyond all creatures,
Thee.

Christina Rosetti

ENCOUNTERING STILLNESS

Dominic Cogan

Encountering the sacred involves a stepping beyond the thin surface of experience we call reality. We don't necessarily need special objects or places set apart to encounter the sacred. The quality of our attention is the key. Creating the necessary conditions, allowing stillness to emerge, the mind is invited to slow down. Attention settles, awareness becomes sensitised to things we miss when the body is very active and the mind is cluttered with thinking. Slowing things down enough, we may receive an intuition of the sacredness of this experience of being alive.

Meditation

Inviting you now to come into a stillness of body and mind. Resting on the breath as it quietly flows in and out of the body. Observing all those points of contact between the breath and the body whether at the nostrils, the chest or perhaps the belly. Sensing also the points of contact between the body and whatever you may be resting upon.

Deliberately switching down the gears,
allowing the awareness to become more attuned,
to an underlying rhythm, **in tune with** the sacred.
This word 'sacred' points to what is only barely known
and barely understood by the everyday busy mind.
Quietly observing our thoughts
simply letting them come and go,
something mysterious may begin to happen.
A sacred stillness may reveal itself,
words become too small to convey the richness of it.
There is a depth to the moment that we might call 'holy'
or as the mystics have called it, 'a calm abiding'.
Out of this sacred stillness wisdom and insight may emerge.

For many of us, this purposeful sitting still can be a challenge.
Restlessness of both body and mind
may seem like barriers to centring ourselves in inner awareness.
Keeping the eyes open and focused on something natural
in your surroundings can help.
Gazing on a flower, a leaf, a stone or a shell
may be a useful aid in helping the mind to settle.
These natural objects can become our teachers.
They appear to us to be material objects that don't move.
But scientists tell us that at the molecular level,
they are vibrating just as we also are.

Beholding them in stillness,
maybe finding an entry point
into the sacred stillness
that pulsates within each of us.

'Do you have the patience to wait till your mud
settles and the water is clear?
Can you remain unmoving till the right action
arises by itself?
The Master doesn't seek fulfilment,
Not seeking, not expecting,
She is present, and can welcome all things.'

Lao Tzu

Evening Is Sacred

Barbara Whelan

For me, evening is a particularly sacred time. As the day draws to a close, silence seems to wrap itself around me like a prayer shawl and I rest in the embrace of its final gift of the day.

The call of the bell
The invitation of the bowl
The cry of the muezzin

Beneath bell, bowl and muezzin
lies Silence

Be still
Open
Wait
Listen

Be still
Be still

Meditation

Sit in a comfortable position, aware of your feet firmly planted on the ground. Ensure that your back is straight but not stiff. Let your neck and shoulders soften and relax. Place your hands on your knees and allow your eyes to close gently, or hold them softly in a downward gaze. If you have a meditation bell or bowl, you might like to sound it to mark the beginning of this sacred time.

Breathing in I am still
Breathing out I open
In, still
Out, open.

Be still
Open
Wait
Listen

Be still
Be still.

Breathing in I wait
Breathing out I listen
In, wait
Out, listen.

Be still
Open
Wait
Listen

Be still
Be still.

Breathing in I touch
Breathing out I am touched
In, touch
Out, touched.

Be still
Open
Wait
Listen

Be still
Be still.

Breathing in I embrace
Breathing out I am embraced
In, embrace
Out, embraced.

Be still
Open
Wait
Listen

Be still
Be still.

The call of the bell
The invitation of the bowl
The cry of the muezzin

Beneath, bell, bowl and muezzin
lies Silence

Be still
Be still.

‘We can only give away to others
what we have inside ourselves.’

Wayne Dyer

Franciscan Contemplation: Sitting with a Tree as Brother or Sister

Br Richard Hendrick

In St Francis, we find one who has passed through the work of meditation and has reached the heights of contemplation. When we examine his contemplative practice, we are given a map that takes in all of creation.

Francis passed from his first prayer of conversion, his first mantra of meditation as it were, which his biographers tell us was, 'Who are you, my God, and what am I?' to the end of his life, when his meditation had become the prayer of creation itself, 'My God and my all!'

Seeing deeply within and beyond, Francis beheld the Divine light of the love of the Creator, holding all things in being and continually pouring itself out in unconditional love for creation. Recognising the common origin of all beings, Francis is invited into the universal song of praise, the very energy by which all things exist. He encounters all as brother or sister. He becomes their voice, their minstrel, their herald, liberating the secret Gospel of creation present in their very being. This too comes to us as graced gift.

Why did St Francis choose the forests and the mountains as one of his preferred places of contemplation? What did the trees teach him? What do trees teach us? If we sit in aware stillness, we are slowly taught by them.

Meditation

Find a tree that you can sit with or under.
Take some time to come to stillness.
Try with open eyes to take in the fulness of the tree.
Watch how it moves in the breeze,
how it sits in the Earth,
how it lets the light shine through its leaves and branches.
Reflecting on our common Divine origin,
begin to simply and internally call the tree brother or sister.
You may like to do this as you breathe in and out.
Realise you are sharing breath with the tree,
you need the oxygen the tree breathes out
Brother/Sister Tree needs the carbon dioxide you breath out.

Ask yourself what lessons the tree teaches you today?
Some of them may be:
To root yourself firmly in the Earth ...
To breathe deep and long ...
To remain in stillness and silence ...
To accept the seasons of your life as they come and go ...
To bend to the winds of change
but never yield your heart to that which is changeable ...

To accept that only by dying to self, will the seeds planted within
grow to new life ...
To reach towards Heaven with all your might ...

Ask yourself:
How would it be to learn these lessons from the trees,
how would your life look?
How open to Divine meaning and love would you then be?

Sit in stillness sharing your breath with the tree until the time of meditation comes to a close.
Offer a moment of gratitude and blessing to finish.
If you can, place your hand on the tree and give thanks for its beauty and wisdom.

Voice of My Soul

The Voice of my Soul is laughing,
joyously filling the space
within and without.
The Voice of my Soul rises from deep within
and sings a song of love.

Laughter is the voice/expression of the soul.
Music is the voice/expression of the soul.
Poetry is the voice/expression of the soul.
Art is the voice/expression of the soul.
Love – it is the ultimate expression.
Prayer, chanting and meditation –
The pathway to the Voice within.

Marsha Eger

Heart Space: Pūrna

Riana Walsh

The Sanskrit word pūrna translates as wholeness, fullness, completeness. It describes a profound felt-sense of oneness and connection – in nature, meditation or yoga. Whether a glimpse or a continuum, this expansive heart-space experience is entire and complete in its beauty and simplicity. Once experienced it is never forgotten.

Meditation

Gently close your eyes.
Receive the breath.
Give your attention to the flow of your breath,
breath flowing in,
breath flowing out.
Feel the breath in your nostrils ... in your throat ... under your collarbones ...
and allow your in breath to gently guide your attention inwards towards your heart space

– not the physical heart but that subtle centre located in the chest area,
a place of inner spaciousness where your inhalation naturally comes to rest.
Let your awareness enter this space inside the heart centre.
Let your breath flow freely and easefully in and out of this area,
breath flowing in,
breath flowing out.
Notice how that inner space of your heart softens and widens with your in breath.
Notice any sensations of expansion, spaciousness within this inner space of the heart.
Incoming breath ... outgoing breath.
Now gently breathe in *from the space in front of you*,
follow the inhalation,
notice how it softly fills the inner heart space.
Now gently breathe out *into the space in front of you*,
follow the exhalation,
notice how it softly fills the space beyond you.
With each *inhalation* bring a warm radiance to this heart space.
Rest your awareness in this radiant space.
Notice how the in breath slowly begins to dissolve.
With each *exhalation* allow that radiance to flow outwards.
Rest your awareness in that space in front of you.
Notice how the out breath slowly begins to dissolve ...

Continue breathing slow, steady, smooth, even breaths in.
Resting your awareness in the inner spaciousness of your heart,
Breathing slow, steady, smooth, even breaths out,
into the space beyond you, resting your awareness here.
Breath flowing in, breath flowing out.
Like the slow rhythmic movement of a pendulum.
Breath flowing in, breath flowing out.
Take time to linger in the fullness at the end of each inhalation,
before it dissipates.
Take time to linger in the fullness at the end of each exhalation,
before it dissipates.
Immerse yourself in a felt-sense of wholeness, completeness, perfection.

Taking time to come out of your meditation,
deepen your inhalation,
feel the breath in your body,
sense parts of the body,
bring your awareness back into your physical body,
exhale,
slowly open your eyes,
savour the effects of your practice.

Heart Space: A Visualisation

Joan Flannelly

'The mind creates the abyss, the heart crosses it' (Sri Nisargadatta).

The heart space transcends this divide and brings us to a place of connection, of unity with ourselves and with others. When we rest with the heart space, we are resting with our true nature – a warm and loving heart.

Meditation

Find a comfortable spot and a posture that helps you feel relaxed and alert. Making sure you are settled and comfortable is a wonderful way to begin to practice.

Take three deep, full breaths and drop your attention into your body.

Notice the solid connection between your body and the surface you are resting on.

Open to the sparkle of sensations flowing through the body.

Contemplate that you are resting on and being supported by Mother Earth.

Invite your attention to simply rest here, grounded on the Earth.
Rest here for a few minutes with your gently breathing body.
Now, bring attention to the heart space – that space at the centre of your chest.
Imagine a candle or an old-fashioned oil lamp in the centre of this space.
As you breathe in,
the flame is lit and gently illuminates the entire heart space.
As you breathe out, the flame dims but remains lit – like a candle at the centre of a cave.
As you move into this practice,
imagine the light, the lamp of the heart, encompassing
both mind and body,
then spreading outwards, touching all beings.
Rest here, with the light of the lamp, in your heart
navigating life by the light of the heart,
rather than the gulf created by the mind.
Connect with your true nature,
walking the path of compassion and wisdom.

When you feel ready, gently release the image of the candle,
gradually shifting your attention back to the breath and to the body.
Your breathing body,
a place and space of possibility.

‘If God could have revealed himself without the world, he would not have created it.’

Meister Eckhart

Hope

Andrea Boudin

Hope is, perhaps, the prevailing attitude that helps many of us to get out of bed in the morning. We hope for goodness, for better circumstances, we might even hope for the gift of hopefulness when things seem dark. We never hope for things to get worse for us: that would not make much sense. Hope arises as a response to crisis or challenge and opens us to new creative possibilities.

Meditation

Try to evoke your experienced sense of hope.
It can be helpful to evoke culturally embedded symbols of hope,
such as a rainbow, a blossoming branch, a Christian cross, a dove or a butterfly.
What does this experience of hope feel like?
What does hope taste like?
What kind of memories arise in the context of hope?

What counter-arguments does the mind come up with, to question your attempt at hopefulness?
Maybe, dwell in or on the emotion of hopefulness for a short while,
feeling and hoping yourself into a brighter, better, more just future.
What are you hoping for today,
and why?

Kindness

Sarah Murray

When asked, on her ninety-second birthday, to share the most valuable wisdom she had gained over her lifetime, my mother offered just two simple yet profound words: 'Be kind.' That's it – just be kind. This meditation is dedicated to the memory of my lovely mother, Philomena.

We are touched by and touch the world. When we show kindness, it is an act of tender care for someone else. A compassionate desire to help or ease the struggle of another, it is a generosity and opening of the heart. It does not have to be anything grandiose. The smallest of simple gestures – a warm smile, kind word, gentle gaze, soft touch – can profoundly effect and touch the heart of another. It can make us feel seen, heard and understood, deeply connected to each other in that moment.

Meditation

Inviting you to recall a moment now when someone showed you kindness.

Recalling where you were, who it was that was kind to you.

What was it they said or did? What did kindness look like?
Maybe it was a simple smile or a nod, a holding open of a door,
a helping hand with something you couldn't manage.
Perhaps it was something more?
Someone who just listened,
who really heard you in a time of need.
Allowing this memory to softly settle in the heart.
Now, tuning into how it made you feel.
Possibly, there is a sense of warmth,
a softness in the body, a sense of being cared for?
Immersing yourself in the ripple effects of your experience.
Holding the memory in your body, heart and mind.
Inviting your whole being to be filled with the resonance of this memory.
Breathing into and out from the heart space.
Allowing it to gently expand.
Bringing to mind now a moment
where you showed kindness to someone else.
Remembering what you said or did,
how you felt afterwards.
Sensing into the resonance of this in the body, mind and heart.
Taking a moment now to set an intention, to make a small act of kindness for yourself,
knowing that to care for yourself is to care for the whole of the world.

When we learn to take care of ourselves, we are better able to take care of others.
Taking this intention of kindness with you throughout the rest of your day.

Leisure

What is this life if, full of care,
We have no time to stand and stare.
No time to stand beneath the boughs
And stare as long as sheep or cows.
No time to see, when woods we pass,
Where squirrels hide their nuts in grass.
No time to see, in broad daylight,
Streams full of stars, like skies at night.
No time to turn at Beauty's glance,
And watch her feet, how they can dance.
No time to wait till her mouth can
Enrich that smile her eyes began.
A poor life this if, full of care,
We have no time to stand and stare.

William Henry Davis

Letting Be

Kathleen Curley-Clarke

The Beatles may have been on to something! 'Being with' whatever comes is a way of being that arises from a wise acceptance of 'what is'. This acceptance to being with whatever is, is not a weak compliance or a sense of giving up. It is a wisdom – a wise acceptance that allows us to be fully aware of what this present moment is offering, and then gives us the opportunity to greet the next moment with wisdom and strength.

Meditation

Let's take a few moments to let ourselves *be*.
Sitting, reclining, lying down. Holding this book.
Let's practise being with this moment.
We don't need to fix or change anything.
We don't need to react, to jump to attention.
We simply allow ourselves to experience
how it feels to let ourselves *be*.
How is the body in this moment?

Gently observe the position of the body.
Notice places where there is a sense of support,
or places where there is pressure or weight.
Breathing in and out,
letting ourselves be with this body in this moment.
As we give time to the body
as it is in the reality of this moment,
we may notice aches and pains or discomfort.
Congratulations!
We have just given ourselves the opportunity to stop.
To notice what *is*.
To *let it be*.
Now, with that awareness and acceptance,
we bring wisdom with us to the next moment.
What does the body need now?
A stretch?
A rub?
Letting ourselves be with the body
allows us the opportunity to get to know what's going on.
To become aware of the reality.
To accept the reality.
To respond with wisdom to the reality.
Really enveloping the body with attention and awareness.
An invisible self hug.
Bringing kindness and wisdom to this body as it is right now.
Sitting or lying here with this book, letting this moment be as it is.

Noticing every ingredient of the reality of this moment.
Giving time to really letting things be is the way,
to learn how best to support, nourish and care for ourselves
as we step into the next moment.
Right now, being with this body in this room in this moment
 – does any wisdom offer itself?
Do you need to yawn? To stretch? To drink?
An extra cushion? Fresh air?
Let yourself *be* in this moment, as fully as possible.
As you turn the page or close this book, remember to be.
Just be.

Letting Go

Kathleen Curley-Clarke

Letting go can seem like an 'all-or-nothing' deal. This can be daunting. If we can soften this idea, to just take opportunities to loosen or release an unnecessarily tight grip on a difficulty, we will discover that little by little, we become more at ease with letting go of whatever doesn't serve us.

Meditation

As you sit with this book, imagine yourself holding a floating helium party balloon.

What sort of grip is necessary?

Having a tight, white-knuckled fist is a total waste of effort! A very light, gentle grip between thumb and forefinger is plenty. The balloon is still here, but our burden of effort is a lot less. We have managed to soften. To let go a little.

Allow that image to fade and now bring to mind the thought of holding an egg in the palm of your hand.

What comes to mind when you imagine using a tight grip on that egg? (Imagination only please! No need for broken eggs!)

If we let go of the egg completely, it falls and breaks.

If we hold on too tight, it gets crushed.

Letting go of a tight hold and allowing something to be supported and held is a manageable balance.

Now simply breathe.

Drawing in the breath, holding the breath, letting go of the breath.

We manage to let go thousands of times every day.

Focusing on the difficulties we feel we 'should' let go of

may cause us to lose sight of our natural ability to just let go effortlessly.

We hold on to regrets, grievances, expectations, disappointments, pain, suffering ...

but by simply softening our grip we will find more ease in our lives.

Drawing in this breath, holding this breath, letting go of this breath.

Congratulations – you've just let go!

As you sit with this book, breathe in and breathe out.

Each time you bring your awareness to your out breath you are cultivating the skill of letting go.

Notice this breath coming in to this moment, then notice this breath leaving this moment.

As you finish reading this meditation, you can let go of the experience. Another opportunity to deliberately, safely and easily practise the art of letting go.

'Behind all names and forms is the one nameless, formless Essence. Behind all sounds, there is the soundless Supreme Silence.'

Sri Aurobindo

Listening

Thomond Coogan

Listening to find out how I am in a world that is heavy with noise.

I am sometimes distracted and overwhelmed by unwelcome noise. This uproots me from knowing who I am, how I really am, or that I need to be less anxious and more in tune with myself. Meditation opens up that inner space of awareness, where I connect with my truths and generally become more accepting and less reactive.

Meditation

We don't need silence to meditate.
This practice works with sound to bring us into a mindful state.
Firstly, adopt a kind and gentle attitude to yourself,
and to the time you give to this practice.
The invitation is to hear what is there to be heard.
There is nothing to achieve other than to be still
and to allow and notice sound as it arises.

All we need to do is allow sounds to come and go.
We do this without naming the sounds,
without creating a story about them,
or passing judgement.
We allow the sounds to come and go as they may.
We stay with the experience of sound, in the moment.
We also notice the absence of sounds – the sound of silence.
Just stay and rest in the gaps between sounds.
Simply observe when the next sound arises.
When the mind drifts off into thinking,
gently return attention to the sounds arising.
This brings us back to the moment,
mind resting in the body,
body in a restful position, where our attention is held by sound.
Notice whether some sounds
seem more pleasant or more welcome than others.
See if it's possible to experience sound as pure sensation,
in terms of volume or vibration.
We may notice sounds from within our bodies,
breathing sounds, or sounds from our bellies.
Other sounds emerge from close by,
more from further away.
Some may be loud, others gentle and low.
Sounds may be experienced
as familiar or entirely new, soothing or disturbing.
Allow your mind to be open and alert.

If you find yourself reacting to sounds,
accept the authenticity of those reactions.
Experience the sounds here as pure sensations
without becoming involved in thinking about them.
Simply smile and allow the sounds to come to you.

At the end of the practice, take a few moments to notice how you feel in your body, thoughts and emotions.
Be grateful for the benefits of your meditation practice and express the wish that those benefits be shared and radiate from you in ever-widening circles.

'There's a magic in the distance, where the sea-line meets the sky.'

Alfred Noyes, 'Forty Singing Seamen'

Loving Awareness: A Visualisation

Joan Flannelly

'And did you get what you wanted from this life, even so? I did. And what did you want? To call myself beloved, to feel myself beloved on the earth' (Raymond Carver).

Meditation

Begin this meditation by dropping into the body,
connecting with the flow of breath
opening into your heart space.
As you are resting in the heart space,
imagine yourself in a place that is safe and comfortable.
This might be a beautiful beach,
a forest glade,
a cosy armchair at home, by the fire.
Invite your imagination to roam freely.
Take a few moments to connect with this place.
Once you feel settled,

bring to mind all the people who have loved and cared for you.
This may include people you love or have loved,
animals,
spiritual figures.
Feel the connection.
Imagine, whoever they might be, coming towards you,
greeting you.
Spend a little time with each one,
receiving their positive regard and well-wishing for you.
These beings love and care for you,
wish for you to be happy.
They are filled with joy to be with you.
As more and more well-wishers join,
they form a circle around you,
enveloping you with their warmth and kindness.
Imagine this outpouring of love
flowing into your heart space,
filling it entirely with compassion and good will.

Rest here, for as long as you like,
bathing in the love and good will that surrounds you.
Acknowledge each being with a gesture of gratitude,
then bid them farewell,
letting them melt into your heart.

When you feel ready, gently release the image.
gradually shift your attention back to the breath and the body,

knowing that your circle of caring is part of you,
always with you,
a locket of love worn close to your heart.

Mindfully Gazing

Sr Stanislaus Kennedy

There are many ways of noticing the world we are part of, ranging from superficial glances to deep appreciation and understanding. This meditation will focus on looking and really seeing each moment as it comes and as it goes, with appreciation. For me, this is the art of mindfully gazing, gazing inward, moving me into the deep and discovering inner strength.

Meditation

Pausing.
Gazing.
Inviting the next few moments to speak to you,
to speak to your heart.
Finding a quiet place to be.
Inviting your back to be comfortable and straight.
Noticing where your feet are placed and becoming aware of them.
Taking a moment to be present.

Gently observing how you are at this moment.
Adjusting your position if necessary.

Becoming aware of your breath.
Do not change your breathing in any way.
After a few moments, noticing the point
when the in breath becomes the out breath
and the out breath becomes the in breath.
Following the movement of the breath inviting you
into a place of rest,
a place of perfect peace at the centre of your being.

Taking a moment to become aware of the Divine presence,
in this present moment.
Inwardly gazing.
Resting in deep awareness of God's presence.

Being with your God in mindful awareness.
Opening your heart, with no judgement.
Gazing with a loving attentiveness,
knowing there is no need to understand anything in
particular.
Resting and becoming still.
Mindfully gazing.
Listening to the small voice of God speaking to you,
in this moment.

Be still and know that I am
Be still and know that I am
Inwardly gazing

Be still and know that I am
Be still and know that I am
Inwardly gazing

Be still and know
Be still and know
Inwardly gazing

Be still
Be still
Inwardly gazing

Be
Be
Inwardly gazing

Moving towards the end of this practice, pause.
Appreciate all the moments of gazing inward
and then gently bring your awareness back
to the experience of your body and your breath.

The Orchid

The orchid gazing on me as I gaze on it
Firmly rooted in the Earth
surrounded by six strong green leaves
Reaching upward in one strong elegant stem
opening its blossom
Beauty and fragility calling me
to find the beauty in my own fragility.
The orchid gazing on me as I gaze on it
Showing off its five lovely petals
varying in size, shape, form and texture
each a different shade of delicate green.
The orchid gazing on me as I gaze on it
Four small uniquely shaped petals at its centre
opening out, revealing to the world
its budding breathing beautiful heart.
The orchid gazing on me as I gaze on it

The heart centre strong and robust
holding everything in place
calling me to listen to my heart
to love with and lead from my heart.
The orchid gazing on me as I gaze on it.
It is the gaze of God, gazing on me as I gaze on her.

Sr Stanislaus Kennedy

Mystery

Síle Wall

Mystery is a word I tend to use quite often these days. It is a word that helps me reflect on life with all its ups and all its downs. For me, being alive is a mystery, taking place moment by moment, along a journey of becoming.

Meditation

Giving yourself the time and the freedom to arrive
into a quiet space.
There is no rush
arriving in your own time and your own way.

Inviting your body to settle itself into a comfortable position,
a position that, maybe, can embody a sense of presence,
presence to this moment in time,
maybe presence to self.

It takes time to move from all the activity of the mind
into the stillness and silence of meditation.
It takes time to move into the mystery of our being,
the mystery of life ... the mystery of my life.

I go to meditation
and sit still.
I pause.
I am arriving
alive and alert.

Becoming present to your body, your alive body,
if you can, consciously relax into this moment of presence,
a moment of awareness.
Maybe noticing a movement in your body,
the gentle movement of breath
as your body breaths in and breaths out.
Your breathing body ... your alive body.

Becoming aware of the natural flow of your breath
in and out, in and out.
Inhale, exhale.

I go to meditation
and sit still.
I pause.
This unique moment of existence

greets me.
I feel its touch,
a gentle wave of presence
touching into mystery.

The mystery of life is this present moment …
inviting me to become present to myself … my unique self.
In the words of Edwina Gately, '… *inviting me to wondrous nothing, there to sit alone in solitude's gaping spaces.*'

Becoming present to myself … body … mind … spirit.

I go to meditation
and sit still.
I pause.
I pay attention
step by step
breath by breath
moment by moment
heartbeat by heartbeat
aware that I am aware
allowing myself to *be*.

'If we are not reborn – if we cannot learn to look at life with the innocence and enthusiasm of childhood – it makes no sense to go on living.'

Paulo Coelho, from By the River Piedra I Sat Down and Wept

Nature and Ubuntu

Niamh Bruce

At the time of being asked to contribute something to this book, I was working on a mindful intervention in Rwandan and Ethiopian schools. Nature is a core component and the African philosophy of Ubuntu is woven deep throughout. Ubuntu teaches us about interconnection, 'I am because we are.' 'I am because the Earth is.' We are more likely to protect the Earth when we are aware that we exist because of the Earth. This is interconnection with each other, but also with the world we live in. This practice can be done sitting in your home or, if you are lucky enough to be able, go out into nature: the garden, park or coast.

Meditation

Let us Begin.
Allow the body to settle, grounding yourself with the anchors of body, breath and/or senses.
Become aware of the chair you sit on, the feet on the floor.

Allow the eyes to gently close, or direct a soft gaze towards the floor.
Be aware of the place you are sitting, the breath as you breathe.
Now, allow your awareness to go beyond
the walls of the room, building, place,
widening your attention to the natural world that surrounds you,
becoming aware of its spaciousness.
Invite an awareness to the layers deep below,
foundations,
Earth.
A living breathing Earth.
Breathing in and out, allowing the Earth to support you.

Becoming aware of a tree, any tree, its shape, size, maybe colour,
notice the connection between you and the tree,
breathing in the oxygen created by the tree,
allowing it to flow through the body, nourishing every cell.
As you exhale, the oxygen has been transformed into carbon dioxide and
the tree is breathing it in.
Breathing in and out, be aware of the connection, the interconnection.
If it is comfortable, invite gratefulness for this gift,
the gift of trees.

Breathing in and breathing out,
say 'thank you' to trees for this life-giving gift,
resting in any sensations of gratitude,
allowing all to be present in the body.

When you are ready, bring your attention once more to the place you are sitting in, the feet on the floor, the clothes against your skin.
Bring this practice to a close, inviting a deep breath.
If it feels comfortable, hold the image of a tree in your gaze as you exhale, stretching the body, and saying 'thank you'.
I would like to invite you, the next time you are out walking, or even if you catch a glimpse of a tree from a window, to notice your breath.
I am because we are. I am because the Earth is.
Thank you for your practice.

Nature as a Teacher

Niamh Bruce

Long before there was such a thing as a 'course in mindfulness' or a 'mindfulness teacher', nature has been teaching us how to be present, has nourished us. In fact, you could close this book and simply stand in nature and ask the question 'How does nature teach me?' Listen to the answer. It will reveal itself if you can just be present.

Let nature teach you. Go to nature and listen. Stand or sit in a position where you can be present with nature. It could be a view from a window, or you could be lucky enough to sit or lie in nature: a field of wildflowers or the shelter of a tree. Nature is the teacher. Your senses are the channels or gateways in which to learn and receive the lessons.

Meditation

So, find your spot in nature.
Allow your attention to drop below the thinking mind and open your senses.
Take it in on a somatic level.

Notice how you feel when you can be present to the colours, sounds and touch of nature.
Notice the sounds that move through nature: wind through the trees, waves crashing or gently approaching the shore,
bees on their search for nectar,
birdsong – there is a symphony awaiting.
Notice the magnificent colours, created and abundant in nature,
inviting your eyes to touch colours and shapes,
beyond the beauty of the most fantastical imagination.
It's real!
Our eyes, the eye of our heart, can touch those colours, shapes and sights.
The smells that consumerism tries to recreate and sell to us,
are freely available in our fields, forests and coastlines.
Go to them.
Experience the touch of grass across your fingertips.
You can almost feel the beating heart of a tree through its bark.
Nothing is so calming and beautiful as to hold a petal so gently between your fingertips that you don't damage it.
It will teach you compassion, patience, gentleness.
If you are lucky enough, a butterfly may land on you, or a ladybird.
Go so quiet and still and that moment will feed your soul.
Going beyond the sights and sounds of noise and busyness
nature is there.

Be present to it.

Close this book and search out nature in any form.
Then become present by bringing your attention to the senses.
Putting the phone away, don't worry about 'capturing this moment'.
It loses its power when we try to 'capture' or imprison nature in one moment.
Nature is moving and dynamic, it is breathing, living.
Flow with it, breath with it, allow it to wash over you.
Surround yourself in nature and be curious to the lessons it is willingly giving us.
If only we would listen.

The Oak Tree

There is an oak I know,
old, battered by storms,
but still standing straight,
the life force strong in it.
I like to lean against it, drawing on its strength,
feeling its rootedness flowing into me.

It asks for nothing in return.
It is simply there,
being a tree.

Julia Cousins

Now Is the Time

Síle Wall

Now is the time. The past has gone. The future has not yet come. By really tuning into this new moment, this now moment, I believe it offers an opportunity to embrace the mystery of existence. It can also generate a sense of aliveness, curiosity and openness to life with its many wonders.

Meditation

Carve out a quiet space for yourself,
at ease with your surroundings.
Life is going on around you and within you.
Gently open to the gift of this new passing moment.
This moment is now.

Welcome this precious moment,
observing how this moment in time
comes, stays and gently moves away.
With the lens of awareness, lean into the rhythm

of one moment following another moment.
This new moment.
This in-between time.

Pause.
Are you noticing how your body is connecting to this moment?
Becoming aware of the grounding presence of your posture?
Greeting and responding to your experience with an openness and curiosity.
The past is gone.
The future has not yet arrived.
Your body is right here.
You are breathing.

Where is your mind?
Maybe noticing the ebb and flow of your inner dialogue?
Give your mind the freedom to be as it is,
allowing sound, thoughts and feelings come
and then letting them go.
The wonder of just being present to life
your life, right now!

In this moment, without having anything to do,
notice how your heart is responding!
Each heartbeat a reminder of life.
Each pulse, a reminder of your presence in this new moment.

Your unique presence.
Alive.
Present to your body as it is right now.
Present to the wonder of your mind.
Present to your loving heart.

If it feels right, and in your own time,
become present to that other space deep within.
Perhaps becoming aware of a deep silence at the core of your being?
Your space – a sacred space, a soul space, a silent space.
A welcoming space.
Allowing yourself to rest here without expectation,
just present to yourself, with yourself.
Savouring these precious now moments,
The past has gone, the future has not arrived.
You are here, now, fully alive, alert and aware.
Breathing in and breathing out.

'Dig inside. Inside is the fountain of good, and it will forever flow, if you will forever dig.'

Marcus Aurelius

Pathway to Awareness

Thomond Coogan

I heard Jon Kabat-Zinn say of meditation, 'Practise as if your life depends on it.' I find it does.

My sister swims throughout the year and never regrets accepting the urge to brave the Atlantic and experience being fully alive and present. I have no such urge, though I have the same drive for deep awareness and oneness with nature. One of my practices is to weave mindfulness into as many aspects of my life as possible.

Even the most seasoned meditators have days when access to the present moment eludes them, and the mind continues to race and wander.

It is good to be conscious that this is perfectly natural; it is what the mind does and is referred to as our monkey or butterfly mind. We cannot force calm on the mind, but we can build pathways to awareness through being mindful of our experience in a given moment. The Buddhist monk Thich Nhat Hanh said, the secret of meditation is to be conscious of each second of our existence.

This may seem like a tall order, but it's not.

Meditation

The invitation is to keep 'the sun of awareness' shining,
and to fully immerse ourselves
in all things as they arise,
even the smallest and most mundane.
Children do this all the time.
We grown-ups have so much to learn from observing little children.
Can you picture yourself as a little child
and then smile at your younger self?
Let the smile be kind and lingering.
If it works better for you to picture another child,
then do so and smile kindly upon them.
Now, can you observe the little child washing their hands
in warm soapy water?
Sense into their absolute focus,
enjoyment,
delight in water and bubbles.
The child is not involved in thinking
but is in the moment,
washing their hands.
Just imagine,
from this very moment,
it is possible to be there for yourself
in that same way.
The 'sun of awareness' will illuminate
any of your daily tasks or experiences.

This is living in consciousness
of what is happening while it is happening.
Even washing your hands,
it is that simple.

At the end of this meditation take a few moments to notice how you feel in your body, thoughts, and emotions. Be grateful for the benefits of your meditation practice and express the wish that those benefits be shared and radiate from you in ever-widening circles.

Let Us Be Still

Let us be still for a few moments
without moving even our little finger
so that a hush descends upon us.
There would be no place to go,
nor to come from,
for we would have arrived in this extraordinary moment.
There would be a stillness and silence,
that would fill all of our senses,
where all things would find their rest.
Everything would then be together in a deep connection.
putting an end to 'us and them', this against that.
We would not move in these brief moments
for that would disturb this palpable presence;

There would be nothing to be said nor done
for life would embrace us in this wondrous meeting
and take us into its arms as a loving friend.

Christopher Titmuss

PEACE

Declan Conlon

Meditation

As you breathe in and breathe out,
allow yourself to be present, present to yourself.
Asking yourself the question,
How am I in this moment?
What emotions, what feelings are present?
And just allow whatever is, to be as it is.
Breathing in, breathing out.
The breath soothing and calming
body, mind and spirit.

Now, asking yourself another question,
What does peace feel like?
Imagining peace.
Noticing emotions and feelings present.
You can't force any answers.

Peace comes and peace goes.
Sometimes it's fleeting,
Sometimes it lasts longer.
Maybe bring to mind an experience of peace.
What was present?
What was happening?
How did you feel?
Breathing in, breathing out.
Resting in this moment.

Peace is not something we can force.
Peace is not something we can chase.
Peace comes
when we let go, and let it be.
Peace comes
when we are grateful for what we have.
Accepting what is.
Compassionate to ourselves and others.

Coming towards the end of this practice
pause,
Allowing yourself to be present, present to yourself
in this moment.
Allowing whatever is, to be as it is
as you go about the rest of your day
living your life as best you can.

Practising Gratitude

Ailish Jameson

Gratitude is an ingrained part of my daily life and when I reflect on being grateful or appreciative, I think of value: what is it I value in my life? It can be the simplest of things: a coat when it is cold, a walk at the beach or a car starting in the morning.

Meditation

Let's begin this practice by recalling a pleasant experience
that you had today or recently.
An experience that you feel thankful for or that you value.
It could be a meeting with a family member or a friend, a
walk on the beach, time in the garden.
Now, reflecting on the qualities of that experience,
what made it pleasant?
What are your thoughts around this experience as you sit
here?

Can you recall any sensations while the experience was happening,
or maybe now, as you sit here remembering it?
What emotions or feelings were present?
Not analysing your experience,
merely calling to mind a pleasant or positive experience
and contemplating it.

What would it be like to say 'thank you' for that experience?
Not clinging on to the experience
or wishing you could experience it again,
simply practising gratitude
for an event, or maybe a person, that was positive.

Practising gratitude:
all it takes is to become aware of the positives in your life,
the people, places and things you value
and simply say 'thanks'.

'We carry inside us the wonders we seek outside us.'

Rumi

Proprioceptive Awareness

Caroline Kelly

A number of years ago I heard about proprioception, and I was amazed to think that at any given moment, without even looking, my brain knows exactly where my arms, legs, toes and fingers are. Like everybody else, I had always been innately conscious of my body's ability to sense its position, movement and balance in space, but I had not understood the biomechanics and how the body relies on sensory receptors in muscles, tendons and joints that communicate with the brain through sensory neurons to provide real-time feedback about body positioning. Even without visual cues, I can walk without looking at my feet while experiencing the changing terrain underfoot, touch my nose or ear with my eyes closed or maintain balance on one leg!

Meditation

Imagine that you are out walking and becoming aware of
how the body moves,
where it is in space.

Experience how this strengthens the mind-body connection.
Focus on bodily feelings, such as the position of the limbs or the way weight shifts,
bringing attention to the present moment, reducing distractions, and eventually quietening the mind.
Find yourself beginning to feel more centred and steady.
Cultivating smooth intentional movements during a mindful walk.
Remaining anchored in the physical experience of the present moment.
Noticing mundane tasks, such as lifting shopping bags.
Proprioception offers the opportunity
to gauge the weight of the bags,
increase or decrease the muscle effort required to lift accordingly,
coordinate the precise grip strength needed to hold a screw-top bottle
while not over- or under-rotating the cap.
Opportunities to practise proprioceptive awareness are all around
inviting a deepening of each present moment of awareness.
Remaining open and curious simple seeing the world through the lens of the beginner's mind.
Cultivating proprioceptive awareness.
Developing a deeper sense of embodiment.
tuning into bodily movement and sensations.
Bringing each new moment fully into life.

Qi Gong: The Healing Power of Nature

Mark Kingham

Qi Gong is an ancient Chinese practice involving movement and breathing. In this meditation, you are invited to simply follow all or any of the movements suggested, in whatever way suits you best. Focusing on a tree, while engaging in its mindful movements is one way of becoming more aware of life all around. It allows us to attune ourselves to the rhythms of the Earth, fostering a sense of unity and harmony with the environment.

Meditation

Whether you are sitting or standing
begin by bouncing the knees.
Just shaking, dropping and raising the knees,
stimulating the blood and energy flow through the body.
Upper body relaxed.
Breathing relaxed.

Bringing attention to the hands, wrists and fingers.
Activating the energy circulation of the body, through the hands,
feeling each finger, bones, empty spaces, sensations.
Dropping into the body.
Slowly, evenly, fluidly, relaxedly
connecting with the energy of the body.
Breathing relaxed.
Body relaxed.

Now, connecting with a beautiful tree.
Body grounded like the tree.
Roots going down.
Trunk strong.
Building a relationship with the tree
lifting the hands
extending the fingers.
I am here like a tree, here with this beautiful tree.

Getting to know the tree.
Relating to the tree.
Lifting the hands, shoulders moving gently
extending the fingers,
moving the hands up along the trunk of the tree and down.
Opening to any sense of communication with the tree.
Not thinking, keeping the attention on feelings, sensations
as the hands move up and move down.

The upper body relaxing, flowing,
moving with the wind.
Feeling into the energy of the tree,
all the way up and down,
from the roots to the branches and leaves
and out from the leaves towards the space above you and around.
Feeling into the presence of this space, the energy of the tree.
Sweeping the arms up and down.
Relaxing the shoulders.
Fluid.
Open to dialogue,
listening to sound,
becoming aware of smell,
feeling of the wind caressing the body.
Life.
Expanding attention to the heart.
Opening the heart centre to communicate with the tree.
Listening.
Receiving.
Breathing in and breathing out,
finish this practice by bringing the palms of the hands together
move them to the centre of the chest
and say 'thank you'.

The Swan

This laboring through what is still undone,
as though, legs bound, we hobbled along the way,
is like the awkward walking of the swan.

And dying-to let go, no longer feel
the solid ground we stand on every day-
is like anxious letting himself fall

into waters, which receive him gently
and which, as though with reverence and joy,
draw back past him in streams on either side;

while, infinitely silent and aware,
in his full majesty and ever more
indifferent, he condescends to glide.

Rainer Maria Rilke

(Translated by Stephen Mitchell)

Quiet

James O'Connell

Quiet. There are generally two dimensions of this experience that exist for all of us. There is internal quiet and external quiet, and for this practice I wanted to explore internal quiet.

Meditation

I invite you to bring awareness to your internal landscape, using your breath as your anchor. It might be quiet already, it might be busy, might be somewhere in between?

There might be very noticeable sensations in the body, a strong emotion or a series of fast-moving thoughts, or none of the above?

Whatever you observe, I invite you to notice how you immediately relate to your internal landscape.

For many of us, especially those who pursue a meditation practice, we long for greater peace, acceptance and compassion – which is a beautiful, fruitful pursuit.

However, very often, in the pursuit of this internal peace, we can begin resisting, criticising where we are right now because we are not where we want to be.

We can unintentionally add to internal noise when we start to wish away sensations, or difficult thought patterns or challenging emotions. I have done this many times and it rarely helps our pursuit of peace.

The irony is that it is through accepting, and not rejecting, whatever is arising for us internally, that we are moving closer to creating space for internal quiet.

Keeping your breath as your anchor, I invite you to return to your internal landscape if your attention has drifted.

Can you give yourself permission to let your emotions or thoughts or sensations be here with you?

What if it is was okay for our internal world to be exactly how it is?

It doesn't mean that we agree with it, or support it, nor do we judge it, but just allow it to be, for a few moments.

How does that feel?

You might notice that there is more quiet within you now after intentionally allowing what is to be here.

The poet Henry Wadsworth Longfellow reminded us that 'For after all, the best thing one can do when it is raining is let it rain.'

When you feel ready, begin to gently move your toes, fingers and body and slowly bring your attention back to this book.

Rest and Digest

Jane Negrych

This meditation works through engaging the breath and our parasympathetic nervous system so that we may move from a space of activation into a state of rest and digest. Rest and digest is the body's process of conserving energy and entering deep relaxation after undergoing stress.

Meditation

Begin by choosing a posture that will make you most comfortable.
This could be sitting on a cushion, kneeling on a stool, lying down or sitting in a chair.
What's most important is
that you are alert, yet comfortable at the same time.
Now, becoming aware of the breath.
As you become aware of the breath as it moves through the body,
see if you can identify any places that feel tight or tense.

See if you can soften around these areas with the out breath,
almost as if the out breath were washing over them
as a gentle wave would wash over a stone in the sea.
Changing nothing with the breath,
allowing yourself to be just as you are,
I invite you to bring your hand up to your earlobes
and gently start to massage the outer, upper ears.
You may like to give your upper ears a soft tug,
apply a small amount of pressure as you massage the ear lobes
with your thumb and index finger in circular motions.
Then moving the fingers and continuing to massage
the middle of the outer ear and finally the lower lobes.
You might notice that your eyes want to close, or stay open –
whatever feels best for you
so you can feel more fully from within.
Now, relax the arms, down.
Let them hang or drape by your side.
Touch in with any residual sensations from this movement.
Breathing in more fully
and as you breathe out, just releasing any tightness or tension.
Now, bringing the palms in front of you and rubbing vigorously,
generating some heat, and then placing a palm over each eye.
With the fingers on the forehead, allow the head to lean forward,
eyes naturally closing in the semi-darkness,m

seeing if you can allow the head to be simply held in the hands.
Letting the breath be a bit more spacious, a bit more soft,
and on the next outbreath slowly moving the hands
from the head down to the heart space.
Placing the hands on the chest with a little overlap of the fingers,
feeling the full surface of the chest.
Letting your hands hold your heart
and your heart hold your hands.
Continuing to breathe longer, smoother, deeper.
With every breath you can feel the chest rising and falling.
Seeing if you can sense the heartbeat,
letting the rhythm of your heart,
the movement of your breath
bring feelings of rest and relaxation.
A moment of pause.
Now, continue deep down into your belly.
Holding your belly in your hands (without judgement).
Allowing your hands to be held by your belly.
Letting the warmth of the hands soothe your belly
and the belly fill your hands.
Resting and relaxing through the breath and the breathing body.
Finishing this practice,
knowing that you can come back to this practice any time you may need to come into balance and feel more at ease and more at peace, no matter what is happening in your life.

'Feelings come and go like clouds in a windy sky.
Conscious breathing is my anchor.'

Thich Nhat Hanh

Right Here, In This Moment

Mary Jennings

'You are neither here nor there,
A hurry through which known and strange things pass ...'
Heaney's 'Postscript' reminds us that when we are present, what is right here has the opportunity to '... catch the heart off guard and blow it open'.

Meditation

Take a moment to settle.
You might notice your feet on the floor,
where you are sitting or lying.
Notice that you are supported,
by the ground, by what you are sitting or lying on.
Let go into that support.
Just have a sense of the whole body here in this moment.

Become aware of your breath,
moving gently in and out of the body.

There is no need for you to make an effort.
The breath breathes itself.
Just that.
Let go into that movement.
Allow this moment to become restful for yourself.
You are here, just now.
There is no rush or hurry.
As you are aware of the steady breath,
you might begin to notice a slowing down,
a gentle slowing down,
a coming into stillness.
Rest there for a while, as best you can.
The mind will wander.
It's what minds do.
Our practice is knowing just that,
being aware of that, moment by moment.
Perhaps it has wandered into the past,
perhaps into the future.
But right now,
gently bring it back to the present.
This breath, this body, this moment.
Settle again on the breath or the body,
as you bring the wandering mind back home.
Become aware of the sense of being alive in this moment,
with nothing to do,
aware of that, just that.
You might like to put a hand over your heart

to bring greater awareness
to that sense of aliveness in this moment.
As you do that,
notice the rise and fall of the breath in the body
as it carries oxygen
to nurture the heart and the whole body.
And you might be aware of the whole sense of that,
of what it feels like to be alive in this moment.
And the next moment
and the next.
Just here, breathing gently.
The mind may wander again,
with many 'known and strange things' passing through.
Simply let them wander off, as they will,
and come back to yourself,
quietly, gently, breathing,
open to the wonder of heart-felt aliveness,
right here, right now.

Sensory Rest

Jane Negrych

This meditation is an invitation to use the sound and texture of water to soothe us when we feel our senses are overstimulated. So, take this practice with you to your favourite blue zone, whether that be a beach, the bank of a river, a running stream or babbling garden pond, and give yourself permission to disconnect from all technology.

Meditation

Begin, by finding a place to sit beside some water.
Once you have found your place,
close your eyes and listen to the movement of water.
As you listen to the water,
try to let go of any concept of waves, or flow, or droplet,
simply notice the texture and nuance of each sound.
Allowing the sounds to arrive at the ears, holding the mind present.
Now, noticing if there are any sound vibrations in the ear

or sensations arising in the body in response to the sound.
Listening to the sound, as you would a piece of music,
simply resting in awareness of the variations of sound.
Also, noticing the *silence* in which sound arises and fades away.
Slowly opening the eyes,
now turn your attention to the shapes and colours of the moving water.
Again, try your best to refrain from conceptualising what you are seeing,
rather noticing with fresh eyes.
Then widening your vision to take in the horizon and sky above,
focus on the act of seeing,
letting go of thoughts, memories, associations, ideas.
Finally, soften the gaze so that you are not fixing your sight on anything.
Instead,
allowing the colours, shapes, sounds
wash over you,
creating a space to rest in the peace that arrives from receiving,
rather than doing.

'A journey becomes a pilgrimage as we discover, day by day, that the distance travelled is less important than the experience gained.'

Ernest Kurtz

Silence the Inner Critic

Thomond Coogan

'Listen to me now ...' is a phrase I remember from childhood that heralded as many pearls of wisdom as cautions and admonishments. We tend to retain certain voices in our heads, some positive, others less so. Sometimes, the harshest voice is that of our own inner critic. This is a practice that helps me to silence my harsh inner critic.

Meditation

Sitting, or lying, in a comfortable position,
I invite you to picture yourself as a small child.
It may help to locate a photograph of your younger self.
Take all the time you need to be comfortable in your chair, on
a bed, or the floor.
Rest there with that image,
allow a slight but authentic smile to spread across and soften
all the muscles of your face.

Give yourself permission to do nothing else but just sit and be there with the image of your young self.
There is nothing else to do, no one to answer to, nothing to fix.
Rest in your safe, comfortable space,
smiling at your younger self.
It is as simple as that.
Sense what it is like to hold your young self in a loving gaze.
Take all the time you need to be still in this gentle and loving way.
Rest in the present moment, being kind and truly centred on your small self.
If it feels right, you might look gently at your young self.
Words may arise to give comfort or advice to your younger self.
Whatever arises,
be still
know that you have only the most loving and gentle intentions for your little self.
Speak to that younger self in a gentle tone.
You are there for yourself as a small child just as you can be for yourself today,
in this moment
with a warm and loving gaze.
Hold that loving, gentle smile.
Stay with this practice for as long as it feels comfortable.

Know that you are wise and can love and care for yourself anytime.
Create time,
make space, smile, and speak to yourself as you would to your younger, smaller self.

At the end of this meditation take a few moments to notice how you feel in your body, thoughts, and emotions.
Keep smiling.
Be grateful for the benefits of your meditation practice
and express the wish that those benefits be shared and radiate from you in ever-widening circles.

Skimming Stones

Caroline Kelly

'I think of how in my most lonely moments, some strange beauty has wandered into my vision or woven its singular song into my ears and I can't help but feel infused by life' (Rosemerry Wahtola Trommer).

There's something poetic about skimming a stone across the water and watching it disappear. It can be a metaphor for releasing worries, casting off burdens and moving forward.

For most of us, skimming stones started as a playful pastime. Now, as an adult, it has become for me a deeply mindful activity that engages all of my senses, from the careful choice of the stone to the art of heft, and the trajectory of the throw, where a good skim will see the stone glide low and smooth over the water before disappearing into the depths.

Meditation

With the stone chosen, take your position at the water's edge.
Find your balance.
Feet grounded, knees slightly bent, body relaxed but poised.
Your breath deepening, aligning with your stance.
In this moment, you are still
a pause before action,
a space between thoughts.

Before the stone leaves your hand,
a quiet act of choosing.
Eyes scanning for the perfect shape, smooth, flat, weight.
Your mind focused on sensation,
the feel of cool stone against your fingertips.
The stone, drawing you fully into the present.

Throwing the stone.
Exhaling as the stone leaves your fingers,
skimming gracefully,
sinking unceremoniously.
Letting it go.

The stone
teaching us to let go,
to embrace the beauty of fleeting moments.
The stone
touching water

creating ripples,
concentric circles expanding,
then – stillness.

Observing all without judgement,
Accepting the moment.

Who Has Seen the Wind?

Who has seen the wind?
Neither I nor you.
But when the leaves hang trembling,
The wind is passing through.
Who has seen the wind?
Neither you nor I.
But when the trees bow down their heads,
The wind is passing by.

Christina Rosetti

Sound and Healing

Simone Meschnig

I invite you to explore the healing potential of your own voice through the practice of humming. This practice can assist you to relax your body and mind.

Meditation

Find a comfortable sitting position somewhere you won't be disturbed for about ten to fifteen minutes.

First of all, connect with the beauty of your breath.
Become the silent witness of your body breathing.
Become aware of the subtle movement of your in breath and your out breath.
You might be able to hear the sound of your breath.
Perhaps it sounds like a gentle breeze or the sound of the ocean.
Just listen with curious ears.

Now, drop your jaw a bit with your lips still touching each other
as if you have a ball of light in your mouth.
Allow your breath to become hearable with a humming sound.
It doesn't need to be a loud or a long sound.
You can also change the sound from lower to higher humming, if you like.
Feel at ease with this practice.
Now feel this humming sound resonating in your mouth, throat, head, chest and other body parts.
Enjoy this internal sonic massage with the humming sound of your own voice for a couple of minutes.

Now, allow the humming sound to slowly come to an end.
Enter the space of silence for a few minutes.

Reflect on how you feel.
You can hum anytime to yourself
whenever you feel you need a 'humming hug'.

Statio

Sr Stanislaus Kennedy

In the monastic tradition, there is a practice called statio*, which means stopping one thing before beginning another. I find this space 'in between' an invaluable refuge, a sacred pause. It connects me to an imperceptible moment in life, where I can let go of what came before and enter fully into what comes next.*

Meditation

Taking a few moments to slow everything down.
Pausing
Stopping all activity.
Notice how your body is experiencing this slowing down.
Inviting your body to release any tension or worry.
Inviting your body to relax.

Moving your attention to focus on your breathing.
Notice that breathing is happening.

The in breath, the out breath.
Becoming aware of a space between the inhale and exhale.
A new moment.
A sacred pause.

Pausing
Stopping.
Embracing *statio*.

Entering fully into this transitional moment,
a fleeting moment.
Becoming aware of moving gently
from one moment to another moment,
one activity to another activity.
Discovering a new kind of presence in this 'in between' time.
A threshold.
A refuge.
A sacred pause.

Breathing in this transitional moment
And as you breathe out opening to possibility.
Breathing in.
Breathing out.
Inviting peace into this 'in between' moment,
this changing moment,
this ordinary moment.

Becoming aware of how one moment yields effortlessly to another.
A sacred pause.

Connecting to the sacred moments punctuating your day.
Becoming aware of a new sense of presence
in this threshold moment,
this 'in between' moment.
As you continue to breathe in and breathe out
Welcome this new moment,
Embracing *statio* with gratitude.
A sacred pause.

Moving towards the close of this meditation
sense the gentle rhythm of your breathing,
your constant companion.
Follow the cycle of your breathing.
Take a few deep breaths in and then out.
Slowly become aware of the environment surrounding you,
inviting the unique, sacred moments you experienced
to ground you in a present moment experience.

Gitanjali 69

The same stream of life that runs
through my veins night and day runs
through the world and dances in rhythmic measures.
It is the same life that shoots in joy
through the dust of the earth in numberless blades of grass and
breaks into tumultuous waves of leaves and flowers.
It is the same life that is rocked in the ocean-cradle
of birth and of death, in ebb and in flow.
I feel my limbs are made glorious by the touch of this world
of life. And my pride is from the life-throb of ages
dancing in my blood this moment.

Rabindranath Tagore

Today: Morning Is Sacred

Barbara Whelan

'Waking up this morning I smile. Twenty-four brand new hours are before me. I vow to live fully in each moment and to look at all beings with eyes of compassion' (Thich Nhat Hanh).

Each morning I open my window, breathe in and bring to mind the words of this quotation. They have become my morning prayer, and a hymn of thanksgiving for the gift of today.

Meditation

Take a moment to settle into your body, adopting a position that is both relaxed and alert. Allow your back to be straight but not stiff, your head to rest gently on your neck, and place your hands on your knees. You might like to turn your palms upwards in a gesture of invitation and receptivity. Let your eyes close gently or hold them softly in a downward gaze. Take a minute to sense into your own inner dignity and then allow yourself to 'fall awake'.

Breathing in I bow to this new day
Breathing in and breathing out
In and out

Breathing in I awake to this new day
Breathing in and breathing out
In and out

Breathing in I smile at this new day
Breathing in and breathing out
In and out

Breathing in I embrace this new day
Breathing in and breathing out
In and out

Breathing in I give thanks for this new day
Breathing in and breathing out
In and out

Breathing in I send compassion to this new day
Breathing in and breathing out
In and out

Breathing in I see my compassion
as a wild flower
nestled in a tiny crevice

softening a harsh landscape
Breathing in and breathing out
In and out

Breathing in I bow to this new day
Breathing in and breathing out
In and out

Waking up this morning I smile. Twenty-four brand new hours are before me. I vow to live fully in each moment and to look at all beings with eyes of compassion.

Alleluia, Alleluia, Alleluia

Touching Our Inner Stillness

Br Richard Hendrick

In the Christian tradition, we don't speak of practising contemplation so much as being contemplative, that is reordering our lives and our practice such that Contemplation, which is a Divine gift, may happen. One may see it as a cultivation of the garden of the heart that creates the ideal conditions for the flower to bloom. Contemplation itself is, as Saint Gregory the Great called it, the gift of an inner silence and stillness impregnated with Divine love. In this understanding, meditation prepares the practitioner to receive the grace of Contemplation. This meditation allows us to recognise the stillness that is already at the centre of our being.

Meditation

Sitting in a comfortable but alert position,
with hands resting on the lap open palmed
take a moment to settle yourself for this time of meditation.

Resting for a few moments in the awareness of the breath,
the constant ebb and flow of in breath and out breath.
Breathing not just with mouth and nose but with every pore of the skin,
from the soles of your feet to the crown of your head.
Touching the breath with awareness,
touching stillness, beginning with the stillness of the body.
As you watch the rise and fall of your breath
try and centre your awareness on the point where
the in breath becomes the out breath
and the out breath becomes the in breath.
Notice the point of absolute stillness that exists there momentarily.
It is a hinge point around which the cycle of your breath revolves.
If any distraction arises simply return to the breath,
resting in this point of absolute stillness between in breath and out breath.
You are not trying to feel anything or to image anything.
If images or sensations arise,
simply notice them and return your awareness to the point of stillness.
As you rest in the still point,
aware of your feet upon the floor, your back against the chair, your hands upturned,
you can say inwardly 'I have a body, but I am more than my body.'

All the while keeping the point of awareness fixed
upon the still point at the centre of the cycle of your breath.
If emotions or thoughts arise,
you can say inwardly, 'I have feelings or I have thoughts
but I am more than my feelings or my thoughts.'
All the while centred on the still point between the in breath and the out breath.
If your mind needs something to hold onto as well as the breath,
you may like to repeat inwardly the verse from Psalm 46,
'Be still and know that I am God.'
After a few repetitions this may be reduced to simply,
'Be still and know,' or even just, 'Be still.'
For the duration of the time remaining, stay with the stillness and, if necessary, the verse.
Holding to this awareness,
you are choosing to be present and open to the presence of the Divine
from which the present moment arises
and in which you live and move and have your being.
You are choosing to dwell in a contemplative stance,
this is the beginning practise upon which readiness for Contemplation is built, awareness of the point of contact between you and the Divine,
between you and the present moment,
between you and the inner stillness that exists
always between the in breath and the out breath.

As your time of meditation begins to draw to a close,
slowly begin to be aware of the full cycle of your breath following the full path of the in breath and out breath.
Allowing your focus to widen slowly,
you may take in once again your feet upon the floor, your back against the chair, your palm's held upward.
You may like to take a moment for thanksgiving, offering gratitude that you have the space and time to touch this stillness and to open yourself to Divine love.
Then as your practise time draws to a close you may like to make a ritual gesture such as a bow, a prostration or the sign of the cross as you move into the rest of your day.

'Doing nothing is better than
Being "busy" doing nothing.'

Lao Tzu

Unfolding

Deirdre Dowling

Over time, through finding my own style of practice using the breath as my guide, I've been unfolding in myself: peeling back layers until I've reached into the centre of my being, my 'heart space' – a place where I sit with my soul and deep compassion flows for self and others.

Meditation

Bring yourself into a comfortable position.
Maybe, sitting or lying down.
Eyes gently closed, hands resting.
Begin by taking three deep breaths,
maybe, counting four for the in breath and five for the out breath
– whatever you are comfortable with.
Taking your time to observe the sounds around you.
The atmosphere.

Asking yourself a question, *How am I, now?*
Checking in with your energy level,
your body for sensations,
observing the thoughts,
watching them come and go.

Now, letting the question move away into the distance.
Inviting the body and mind to settle.
To soften.
Connecting with the breath.
Allowing the breath to find its own rhythm.
Observing its gentle rise and fall.
The breath is a ticket for this journey of unfolding
bringing you to the centre of your being.
Feel your breath.
Hear your breath.
Know your breath.
Your breath journeying with you into your heart space.
A space where only you can go.
A space where compassion flows.
A space where you can be still,
knowing you are loved.
A space where you can see things in a different way.
You may get pulled away by thoughts sensations, feelings,
but the ticket is in your pocket.
Your breath.
Your breath

accompanying you
back into your heart space,
where you can sit.
Surrounded with kindness and compassion.
Your soul space.
When you're ready
bring the awareness once again to the rise and fall of your breath.
Take a few deep breaths in and out.
Stretching the body gently.
Congratulate yourself for giving time to this journey.
May you take compassion and peacefulness into the rest of your day.

Waiting Without Expectation

Colm Madigan

We spend much of our lives seeking to fulfil agendas – agendas that we have set for ourselves or responding to those set by others. While lifestyle may be of our choosing, circumstances may not. Plans, promises, hopes, fears, anxieties and regret may dominate and dictate our lives. To sit in silence, abandoning all expectation, opening our heart, receptive, surrendering, just being, is a freedom not easily achieved, but provides moments to be welcomed and cherished when we experience them.

Meditation

Sitting silent and still.
Stepping into silence for a short time.
Stepping away from the grip of expectation and demand.
Surrendering all expectations, thoughts and desires.
Inviting calm to hold us.
Calm to enfold us.
Asking for nothing.

Seeking nothing.
Aspiring only to be present to the grace of the moment,
in our meditation experience.
Moments of
joy, celebration,
perhaps sadness, stress, anxiety.
Present with an open heart
a receptive heart,
a trusting heart.
Moments to be welcomed.
In silent stillness
opening to the presence of the Spirit.
Inviting the Spirit into our lives.
Seeking no outcome, no expectations, results or achievements.
Present in silent surrender,
alone, in our vulnerability.
Waiting and receptive.
Waiting without agenda.
Waiting without expectation.
Moving out from this short meditation practice, back into a world of agendas, patiently trusting ourselves and believing in the slow work of God.

'Do nondoing,
Strive for nonstriving,
Savour the flavourless,
Regard the small as important,
Make much of little,
Repay enmity with virtue;
Plan for difficulty when it is still easy,
Do the great while it is still small.'

Lao Tzu

Working with Resistance

Barry Lee

One of the attitudinal foundations of mindfulness is allowing. If you have participated in a mindfulness course, you have probably heard this advice: 'When you practise, just allow each moment to be as it is.' We hear those words and it sounds so easy, but in reality it's very challenging.

Often, when I sit there is something in my experience I really don't want. And a little part of me wants the meditation to 'fix' it. I might feel irritable or stressed or foggy or insecure, and I go to my cushion and I sit ... sometimes with a hidden agenda of wanting to get rid of this difficult experience. I don't want to feel this way ... I want to feel peaceful and calm and happy instead! It never works! Why? Because I'm not allowing this moment to be as it is. I'm resisting my present moment experience. I'm fighting with myself.

Meditation Practice – Embodying Resistance

Make a tight fist with one hand and keep it clenched.
You could imagine that this tight fist is embodying physical, emotional or mental discomfort.
Imagine that this tight fist is scared and feels that it needs to stay clenched.

Don't rush to read the next line.
Perhaps close your eyes and sit with this feeling for a moment or two.

Now, with your other hand, try with all your might to open the clenched fist.
Your other hand really wants the discomfort to go away.
It wants to fix. It thinks it is helping. It says, 'this is not okay!'
Notice what happens.

When I practise this myself, I notice that my clenched fist tightens up even more. Why? Because I'm resisting and as the psychologist Carl Jung once observed, 'what you resist will not only persist but will grow in size.'

So now I'll invite you to try a different approach.
The clenched fist is still here but this time we are not in the mode of fixing.
Allow the clenched fist to rest in your other hand.
Your other hand embodies mindfulness and compassion.

In a soothing voice, your other hand says, ‘It’s okay … This is okay … You are okay as you are.’
Rest with this for a while and notice what happens.

I notice a softening.
The clenched fist doesn’t relax *fully* but it’s easier.
There is more space.
The suffering caused by resisting drops away. I can take a breath.

When you practise, it might be helpful to remember this exercise, especially if you are sitting with some discomfort.
As best you can holding your discomfort with mindfulness and compassion.